Prayers Mommy Prayed After You
After You
A 21 Day Devotional

Prayers Mommy Prayed After You
A 21 Day Devotional
By
Genté Shaw

Sadé Rose Publishing Co.
Portland, Oregon
SRPublishingCo@gmail.com

Prayers Mommy Prayed After You
A 21Day Devotional

Paperback ISBN: 978-0692838716
Printed in the United States
10 9 8 7 6 5 4 3 2 1 0

This collection of prayers is first dedicated to my Heavenly Father, the one and only Living God. Thank you for loving me and entrusting to me our beloved daughters. I am forever grateful to You.

∞

To my husband, Daniel Shaw. Because you chose to walk with me through this life's journey, I am a wife and mother. Our marriage consistently reminds me of Christ. I am privileged to love and to serve you.

∞

To our girls, Chloé Christine and Nylá Rose. The loving bond we share is truly God given. I pray that my life points you to Christ, inspires you to live and motivates you to love. May you two always be strong and courageous, and exhaust God's perfect will for your lives.

∞

To my Granny, Mary Lewis and my mother, Cynthia Traylor, thank you for teaching me to pray. May God continue this legacy.

Prayers Mommy Prayed After You

A 21 Day Devotional

~Author's Opening Thoughts~

"The littlest feet make the biggest footprints in our hearts." (Unknown author)

These are words of encouragement from one mother to another. This little book of love is for mothers during a critically vulnerable phase of motherhood, the postpartum phase. It is filled with simple, yet precise prayers and words of affirmation.

Before praying, I encourage you to enter into God's presence with praise and gratitude. Adore Him, because He and He alone is worthy of our praise. Make mention of feelings of uncertainty and of doubt, ask for forgiveness for your limited abilities, and allow Him to escort you to a mindset of peace, joy, and confidence in your role as a mother. Add to the prayers I have shared within these pages, and tailor them to be the remedies to your needs.

Day 1
I Have Been Gifted

"Children are a gift from the LORD; they
are a reward from him."
Psalm 127:3 NLT

You have just entered into a non-judging
zone, so let's be honest here. Once we arrived
home from the hospital, I realized our
family had grown by one. An adorable,
innocent, and helpless, one. I was
bombarded with questions like: "Can I
handle this? Do I have what it takes? Are
we financially secure? Is there enough of me
to go around?"

Are you able to identify with these
questions? Regardless of the seemingly
never-ending questions or the circumstances
that have brought you or your family to this
place, your new little one is a GIFT from
God. It is His good pleasure to assist you,
your baby, and your family in adapting to
the daily challenges of life. He has and is
continuing to help my family and I dance to
our new rhythm of life. It is a beautiful
thing.

Pray this:

Father God, I ask you to renew my heart and my mind by your word. Help me to see my child as a gift from you. Strengthen me and equip me to be the best mother I can be to (say the name of your child or children). I receive your strength now. In Jesus' name, Amen.

Day 2
My Joy is My Strength

"... for the joy of the Lord is your strength."
Nehemiah 8:10 KJV

After having a baby, our hormones may be in complete disarray. One minute you are doing great, and as soon as someone asks, "How are you doing?", the tears begin to flow. In addition, you are often unable to give an exact reason for the tears. This seemingly fortifies the feeling of inadequacy.

Let's put things into proper perspective. Hormonal imbalance is a natural part of the postpartum phase, so be kind to yourself. Be sure to acknowledge your feelings and thoughts then share them with someone who you know loves you, and more importantly, speak them aloud to God. If need be, cry, then let out a gut-shaking laugh. Yes, in that order! I ask God to cover you, so that the enemy of your soul will not be able to intensify or prolong this natural phase. Sis, you got this!

Pray this:

Lord, I come before you in the spirit of truth, with all that I am and all that I am not. I ask that you remove from me the spirit of heaviness, and bring my emotions and thoughts into divine alignment with your thoughts toward me. I decree that I am fearfully and wonderfully made, in your image and likeness. (Psalm 139:14) May your joy be my strength in this place. In Jesus' name, Amen.

Day 3

I have a Sound, Stable Mind

"For God hath not given us the spirit of fear; but of power, and of love, and of a sound mind."
2 Timothy 1:7 KJV

Whatever concerns you may have regarding being isolated, your family dynamics, your health, and or your finances to name a few, I encourage you to cast them upon the Lord and to fear not. Fear is simply false evidence appearing real. Your concerns are real and valid however, God is GREATER and none of this (your life at this time) catches Him by surprise. In fact, it's all part of the plan. Do not be dismayed, for He has not called you to be a prisoner of fear, but of faith. All that concerns you, concerns Him, so believe it is going to work out for your good in due time.

Pray this:

Thank you Father for blessing me and my family as you have. In this place I choose to activate my faith and to believe your Word. I declare that you have not given me the spirit of fear. I decree that I will live in your power, by your love, and I will make sound decisions. I have a sound, stable mind! I trust you to resolve my concerns, Father. I exchange worry for your peace. In Jesus' name, Amen.

Day 4

My Steps are Ordered by God

"Trust in the Lord with all thine heart; and lean not unto thine own understanding. In all thy ways acknowledge him, and he shall direct thy paths."
Proverbs 3:5-6 KJV

Whether this is your first child or an additional one, bringing home a new baby requires every aspect of your home life to adjust. This is to be expected, yet it is easier said than done. As moms, it is our responsibility to manage our homes. (Read Proverbs 31:15, 21, 27) Here is where we should ask for help from those around us. You are not superwoman and need not feel meager because you need assistance. Our word for this season is DELEGATE! All hands on deck, assisting with cleaning, laundry, and even cooking. "MOManager" is a good title, for we are called to manage the home, not to care for it completely alone. Now ask God for his counsel, and a course of action as to how you are to maintain your home and family.

Pray this:

Father, you are a God of family and order. Help me and my family to adjust to (name of your baby) in our daily lives. We render ourselves to you and ask for your guidance. Help us to be sensitive to your voice, to quickly recognize what you desire of us, and to respond to you with swift obedience. In Jesus' name, Amen.

Read Romans 12: 1-2 MSG

Day 5
I Am Truly Beautiful

"Yet God has made everything beautiful for its own time..."
Ecclesiastes 3:11 NLT

Has someone genuinely commented, "you are beautiful", but moments later, you look in the mirror and you don't see the beauty? Yes, your body has experienced a vast amount of changes during and after pregnancy. Skin pigmentation, stretch marks, swollen nose, hands and feet can be a few. However, these changes do not negate God's truth about you. You are BEAUTIFUL, inside and out. If there are things about your body you desire to improve, you can do it. Make a plan of action, and once you have the doctor's approval, execute the plan. For now, take time to write down positive qualities about yourself (you can have family and friends assist you with this). Then, review those qualities daily. So often, we wait for others to point out the beauty in us. Today, I am challenging you to see yourself as God sees you.

Pray this:

Lord, you are the potter and I am the clay.
Everything that you created, you called good.
Therefore, enable me to see myself as you see
me and enable me to love myself with your
love. Help me to be aware of my emotional
and physical health, and to make decisions
that will allow me to have continual health.
In Jesus' name, Amen.

Day 6
I Make Time For God Each Day

"As the deer longs for streams of water, so I long for you, O God."
Psalms 42:1 NLT

Living life from day to day, cooking, cleaning, nursing, and caring for yourself, your husband (if married), and other family members, may cause you to feel distant from God. You may often ask, when will I have the time to pray or to read my Bible or sit quietly and listen for God's still, small voice? Believe me, as Christ's followers, we all have asked similar questions and have felt distance between ourselves and Him. We must remember that God is always with us and promises to never leave us. The truth is, we become too busy, however He's never too busy. Be authentic before Him and give Him your heart. He can handle it. God is eager to satisfy your thirst.

Pray this:

Father, Your name "Emmanuel" means "God with us." It's who you are. Please forgive me for my tardiness and restore me to my rightful place in you. I seek to be close to you. James 4:8 KJV says, "Draw nigh to God, and he will draw nigh to you..." So, I set my affection upon you, oh Lord. Satisfy my soul as only you can. Lead me into quality time with you throughout my day, as in a spiritual rendezvous. I long for your presence. In Jesus' name, Amen.

Day 7
I Am Intentionally Bold and Courageous

"Now it came to pass on the third day, that Esther put on her royal apparel, and stood in the inner court of the king's house, over against the king's house: and the king sat upon his royal throne in the royal house, over against the gate of the house. And it was so, when the king saw Esther the queen standing in the court, that she obtained favour in his sight: and the king held out to Esther the golden sceptre that was in his hand. So Esther drew near, and touched the top of the sceptre."
Esther 5:1-2 KJV

The book of Esther is epic. If you have not read it, I recommend you do so in your spare time. "Spare time? What is that?", you may ask. Again, we are talking about being intentional, and it may be easiest to listen audibly to the story via The Bible application. My point is to highlight the fact that this particular Biblical account vividly depicts intentionality and courage; and it is a depiction of our relationship with God, the King of Kings. Esther and her people, the

Jews, were scheduled to be annihilated by the king's right hand man, Haman. To prevent such a heinous crime, Esther, forgetting all formalities, went before the king unannounced to vindicate her life and that of her people. I admire her boldness! In fact, as mothers, we have a boldness and tenacity that we ourselves may not have recognized, regardless of our personality types. You and your family may not be at risk for natural annihilation, but know that there is a spiritual struggle for our souls. So here's where we become intentionally courageous and go boldly before God's throne on behalf of ourselves and our families.

Pray this:

Father, you know what I have need of before I even ask (Matt. 6:8), yet you encourage me to come boldly before your throne of grace. (Heb. 4:16) So, here I am asking that you cover and protect my family from dangers seen and unseen. Make us aware of your presence and sensitive to your voice. Strengthen our faith and hope in you that we may be steadfast and unmovable. I trust you, Father. In Jesus' name, Amen.

Day 8

I Am Focused on Greatness

"But seek ye first the kingdom of God, and
his righteousness; and all these things shall
be added unto you."
Matthew 6:33 KJV

Recalibrating life into focus since your new
baby's arrival may be challenging, but it's
necessary. Your good efforts should be made
toward your priorities and not toward
random busyness. Have you heard of the
saying, "good is the enemy of great"? All that
God has for you to do is great. You do not
have to just take my word for this. Christ
said, "Verily, verily, I say unto you, He that
believeth on me, the works that I do shall he
do also; and greater works than these shall
he do; because I go unto my Father" (John
14:12 KJV).

Pray this:

Father, you knew me before time began. Today I ask you to bring me into focus and reveal to me your greater plans for my life. Philippians 2:13 KJV says, "For it is God which worketh in [me] both to will and to do of his good pleasure." Thank you Father for strengthening me where I am weak and mending all brokenness within me. Give me peace and courage to start and to complete the tasks you have for me. In Jesus' name I pray, Amen.

Day 9
I Am Grateful For All Things

"In every thing give thanks: for this is the will of God in Christ Jesus concerning you."
1 Thessalonians 5:18 KJV

So often we forget the direct implication of this scripture; "In *every* thing...". When things are going well for us, it is easy to be thankful and have a pleasant disposition. However, when we are stretched by life's struggles and disappointments, we often react with sadness and self-pity, and then we become angry and defensive toward God and those around us. I am learning that God is extremely concerned with making us our best selves, which we can liken to the action of sandpaper. He uses struggles and disappointments to bring the best out of us. So instead of reacting, let us respond with thanksgiving and gratitude, regardless of the state in which we find ourselves.

Pray this:

Oh Lord, I need you now. Please forgive me for my negative attitude and remove it far from me. Renew in me a right spirit that I may see your hand at work in all I experience. Help me be thankful in the difficult times, although I may not be thankful for the difficult times. In Your son, Jesus' name I pray. Amen.

~After you pray this prayer, your thoughts are your responsibility. God's grace is with you! Nonetheless, you have to intentionally refute negative attitudes and thoughts, then quickly replace them with positive ones.

Day 10
I Choose To Speak Life

"She opens her mouth in [skillful and godly] wisdom, and on her tongue is the law of kindness [giving counsel and instruction]."
Proverbs 31:26 AMP

Have you ever said something you wish you could snatch back or peel away from the atmosphere? You did not mean it, but it "just came out" in "that moment". Oh, how I know, we are human and we are surely fallible. God knows we are not perfect and He does not expect us to be; however, as gatekeepers of our homes and mothers of our children He expects us to speak life. Instead of swearing or putting negative labels on your older son or daughter, be intentional to pause and collect yourself, then address the situation specifically for what it is. Use it as a teaching moment. Say what you would like to see, or hold your tongue and give grace. Because you are your child's mother and more importantly because words have power, your child will believe whatever YOU say about him or her.

Pray this:

Lord, I love (say your child or children's names aloud). Please give me your patience, that I may respond in a way that pleases you when my patience is thin. Help me to know when and how to apply the rod of correction (Proverbs 22:15) and when to extend grace and mercy. Enable me to instill your truth within (name of child or children) so when they are older, they will love and follow you with all their hearts. In Jesus' name I pray, Amen.

Day 11

All Things Work Together for My Good

"And we know that all things work together for good to them that love God, to them who are the called according to his purpose." Romans 8:28 KJV

I have read and quoted this scripture countless times, however, it was not until recently that I actually understood it. It is a declaration of faith because it begins by stating, "And we know...". What a bold introduction! Now, when I read this, I cannot help but to read as if it's in all capital letters, with an exclamation point. It revives my hope and stimulates my faith when I am experiencing everything but goodness. Let this passage remind us that God is using everything, the good and bad days, to perfect us into His divine image. And ultimately, we will come forth likened to pure gold, because we love Him and we are called according to His purpose.

Pray this:

Father, open my eyes that I may discern your work in my life. Empower me to give you my whole heart, the core of who I am. I desire to trust you whether I sense your presence or not. Anchor a certainty deep down within my heart that all things in my life are working cohesively to bring me to the destination you call good! Strengthen me so that in bad times, I may keep the faith to stand and experience greater fellowship with you, even while suffering. And Father, remind me in the good times that it is YOU who sustains me, so that I may remain humble at your feet. In Your Son, Jesus' name I pray. Amen.

Day 12

God's Doing a New Thing

"Remember ye not the former things, neither consider the things of old. Behold, I will do a new thing; now it shall spring forth; shall ye not know it? I will even make a way in the wilderness, and rivers in the desert."
Isaiah 43:18-19 KJV

God's word is true, but humans often lie. Doubt man but never doubt God. Regardless of what your present situation looks like, trust and believe God because you are in your new era. The enemy of your soul is trying to deceive you into thinking you are going down an old path, simply wandering without a divine destiny. But I speak to your spirit. Be bold and courageous, and stand firm in your faith. God is doing a new thing in you, and in every aspect of your life. At the onset of defeating thoughts, say aloud, "devil, you are a liar!!!" You may have to say it aloud several times until you convince yourself, and that is okay. Then, decree the word of God, by saying the scripture above. It takes faith to please God. By your faith, you are walking in your new era!

Pray this:

Oh Lord, thank you for hearing my prayers
and answering me! I bless you for my NEW
era! Thank you for making a way out of no
way and opening up new opportunities for
advancement for me and my family
members! Continue to satisfy our souls,
Father, that we will be like trees planted by
the river of living waters, bearing fruit in
our season. Our leaves will not wither, and
whatsoever we do shall prosper. (Psalm 1:3)
In the name of Jesus', Amen.

Day 13

God's Will Is the Frame of my Life

"...Yet I want your will to be done, not mine."
Luke 22:42 NLT

Is your faith on trial right now? Are you being tested in an area of life that's sensitive to the touch, so to speak? Do you need to forgive someone or yourself, or need to walk away from an unhealthy relationship or job, or relinquish your will for God's will regarding a situation? These are easier said than done, I know. Elisabeth Elliot said it best, "The fact that I am a woman does not make me a different kind of Christian, but the fact that I am a Christian makes me a different kind of woman."

The difference is, as a follower of Christ, we are expected by Him to be a reflection of Him to non-followers. He holds us in high esteem, just as you should hold your children. For instance, when I instruct my five year old daughter to do something, I do not care what her peers may do. She is to do as I asked, with no negotiating. God has given us free will. When we will ourselves to follow Him, He knows that we trust Him wholeheartedly and submit to His will. He knows what is best for us, in spite of what we feel. Let His will be the frame of your life.

Pray this:

Thank you Father for my life. Please forgive me for resisting your will. Give me your heart and mind for my life that I may fulfill your preordained purpose for me. Not my will, but your will be done in my life, in my family, and in all that concerns me. In Jesus' name I pray, Amen and Amen.

Day 14

Christ Has Prayed for Me

"But I have prayed for thee, that thy faith
fail not: and when thou art converted,
strengthen thy brethren."
Luke 22:32 KJV

Are you feeling a little overwhelmed from
the cares of day-to-day life? Or worse, did
you experience something that seems like the
final straw that broke the camel's back?
Even in this moment, fret not, sis. I am here
to remind you, Christ prayed for you in
advance. Because He is eternal, so is His
Word, both spoken and written. His word,
unlike ours, is not limited by time or space.
Take to heart the Word of the Lord; glean
resilience, joy, strength, peace, and all you
need from His Word.

Pray this:

Father, God, I decree that "Thy word is a lamp unto my feet, and a light unto my path" (Ps. 119:105 KJV). I trust that you are bringing all things together according to your divine design. Therefore I relinquish fear, doubt, and self-preservation. I am yours! Cause me to sense your presence in the midst of my present situation and to respond in faith, rather than my feelings. I choose to delight myself in you. In Jesus' name, Amen.

Day 15

I Live in the Moment

"The thief comes only in order to steal and kill and destroy. I came that [you] may have and enjoy life, and have it in abundance (to the full, till it overflows)."
John 10:10 AMP

Have you ever noticed how quickly the years come and go? We remember years by the significant moments that occurred within them. Today I want to encourage you to intentionally live in the moment- be present. Your baby is growing quickly, and time waits for no one; not even a new mommy. So instead of despising the midnight through early morning feeding sessions, the diaper "blowouts" while heading out the front door, and the intense, top of the lungs crying during car rides, embrace the fact that this is your new normal... just for now. These things will change quickly. This realization will lessen your frustration and anxiety, enabling you to find God's joy in each day.

Pray this:

"This is the day which the Lord hath made; [I] will rejoice and be glad in it" (Psalm 118:24 KJV). Father God, I give this day back to you. May your peace envelop me as I choose to be present and attentive throughout this day. Help me to find your joy and to share it with those I encounter. I love you and I bless you for this now, in Jesus' name, Amen.

Day 16
I Am His GOOD Thing (read Proverbs 18:22)

"Who can find a virtuous woman? For her price is far above rubies. The heart of her husband doth safely trust in her, so that he shall have no need of spoil. She will do him good and not evil all the days of her life."
Proverbs 31:10-12 KJV

He loves me. He loves me not. He loves me? He loves me...Not? Because of the physical and hormonal changes you are experiencing, you may have random thoughts doubting your husband's sole dedication and affection for you.

STOP.

Remember that, if your husband loves God with all of his heart and has given his life to Christ, then he is dedicated to God's commandment for Him to love you as Christ loved the church (Ephesians 5:25), selflessly. This is something your husband cannot do in his own strength; instead he has to be empowered by God to properly love you as Christ loved the church. START praying for your husband to have greater submission to

God as well as greater love and affection, solely for you. Pray this daily and especially at the onset of the negative thoughts. This prevents demonic seeds from taking root in your mind and from bearing demonic fruit (such as: insecurity, jealousy, and distrust) within your marriage.

I recommend you share today's devotional with your husband, be authentic and encourage him to do the same. Lastly, pray together specifically over your discussion and marriage.

Day 17

I Am Faithfully Persistent

"And shall not God avenge his own elect,
which cry day and night unto him, though
he bear long with them?"
Luke 18:7 KJV

Have you ever pleaded in prayer for
something? I mean pleaded relentlessly,
much like you look for your keys when
they're misplaced and you are in a hurry.
When you have lost your keys, you turn the
house upside down and inside out to find
them. You are intentional and you are
desperate. What if you prayed faith-filled
prayers with this same intensity? I
remember as a child, pleading to God for my
mother to be delivered from a drug
addiction. I prayed this prayer countless
times, but each time with childlike faith; a
faith that withstood the test of time. After
ten years of praying and trusting God, He
delivered her. I know prayer changes things.
Even if the situation or circumstance itself
does not change, faith definitely changes us,
if we allow it to do so.

Although I was praying for my mother's deliverance, I gained a personal testimony of how good God is even when life is not.

Pray this:

Dear God, set my eyes upon you! You are almighty and all knowing, and I trust that you know exactly what I need and when I need it. So, I give this situation to you (be vulnerable with God and share the details with Him). Lead me as to how I am to pray over this, and give me the courage to remain persistent in faith until change occurs. I decree your perfect will to be done, even if it is not my will. In Jesus' name, Amen.

Day 18

I Am Regaining my Shape and Fitness

"She girds herself with strength [spiritual, mental, and physical fitness for her God-given task] and makes her arms strong and firm." Proverbs 31:17 AMP

There's no doubt about it, our bodies go through some serious changes during pregnancy. This fact has a tendency to diminish our confidence. Come on, let's be honest here. With a little assistance or "The Help" (as I like to call garters, support garments, and the like) we can look and feel great. But we deserve to feel our best in the nude.

Have you ever heard, "skinny girls look good in clothes but FIT girls look great naked!"? If you desire to feel your best in the nude with the lights on, you can! And girlfriend, you deserve to! It's our right! It will take personal dedication and sacrifice, but you can do it. And if you choose not to put in the necessary work, do not despise your sister who does. No money or time for the gym? No worries, there are countless free videos on

YouTube. Get your doctor's approval, then ease your way into getting your fitness back...a few minutes every day makes a difference. You can do this. Please understand me, it is not just about becoming slimmer or solely looking good. More importantly, it's about self-care. If you take care of you, then and only then will you be able to better serve your family.

Pray this:

Oh Lord, this is a personal request. Help me to be consistent in caring for myself. I desire balance- that I may be pleased with myself, both internally and externally. Remove far from me the desire to appear perfect, and grant me your heart and mind towards me that I may be honest with myself and discipline my body into good health. In Jesus' name I pray, Amen.

Day 19

I Change my Thoughts from Negative to Positive

"For though we walk in the flesh, we do not war after the flesh: (For the weapons of our warfare are not carnal, but mighty through God to the pulling down of strong holds;) Casting down imaginations, and every high thing that exalteth itself against the knowledge of God, and bringing into captivity every thought to the obedience of Christ;" 2 Corinthians 10:3-5 KJV

As child, I was sexually violated by an adult male who chose to use his free will as a weapon to destroy my innocence and self-worth. For many years, I buried the images from that night, only to recall them abruptly during joyous occasions. While in high school, I acknowledged this sin done against me before God, and He began the healing process. Now, more than 10 years later, God is still restoring me.

On the day of our older daughter's gender reveal, I was beyond excited to get one step closer to binding with the miracle growing inside me. Then, suddenly, I was burdened with the fear of her innocence being taken, stripped beyond human repair. Although I never stopped praying, the fear was crippling; one that kept me up at night and influenced many of my parenting decisions.

It was not until then, that I realized that my prayers and my soul (mind, will and emotions) were not synchronized. I would sincerely pray God's hedge of protection but, sadly, still imagine the worst. The ungodly images exalted themselves above the knowledge I have of God. I know, without a doubt, that He's faithful, a protector, a comforter and so much more. However, I was not imagining Him to be all of this and more for my daughter. WOW!!! This revelation recently hit me like a ton of bricks, and encouraged me to intentionally change the negative images in my mind into godly images.

Now, I imagine God's guardian angels covering and protecting both of my daughters and making their way prosperous as they come and go. I trust God and take Him at His word. Affliction shall not rise up a second time, for He will bring an utter end to it, according to Nahum 1:9. I know

God did not cause the egregious sin to happen to me; it was the direct result of man's free will. I also know God was there with me (Deut. 31:8) and deeply saddened by its occurrence. (Heb. 4:15) Therefore, I find resolve in knowing that He is making all things to work together for my good. (Rom.8:28) Hence, I am writing this to encourage you.

Identify the ungodly images that plague your imagination, and lay them at the feet of Jesus. Ask God to flood your imagination with godly images, ones which are aligned with His Word. The pain that has scarred you does not have to be a part of your children's stories.

Pray this:

Father, I humbly come before you in spirit
and in truth. Thank you for drawing me into
your presence. I bring before you the
ungodly images that have plagued my
imagination. I cast them down at your feet,
surrendering each one unto you. Remove
even the residue of these thoughts far from
me and increase the volume of your Word
within me. Enable me to meditate and
imagine Your Word being performed in my
life and in the lives of (names of your child
or children). Give me a godly imagination!!!
I receive it now, in Jesus' matchless name,
Amen!!!

(Don't rush. Take the time to praise God and
trust Him to renew you by His spirit.)

Day 20
I Serve Others With Love

"She stretcheth out her hand to the poor; yea, she reacheth forth her hands to the needy."
Proverbs 31:20 KJV

As you become comfortable and well-adjusted to your new baby and your life, you may sometimes feel needy. Needy in the sense of wanting to be affirmed; you want to hear someone say, "You're doing a great job!", or "You're an amazing mother!", or something that lets you know your efforts are being noticed. Your need may also be something different from affirmation. You may need a break, a date, a massage, etc. Consider the scripture above, and with a pure heart, find someone you can bless, someone with a need you can fulfill. With love as your motive, pour out and watch your need will be fulfilled as a by-product of your action.

Pray this:

Father God, thank you for allowing me to recognize my need. I come to you first, Father, to fill this void. I choose to embrace all you have gifted me with and to use it to serve, and to encourage someone else. (1 Thess. 5:11) Thank you for the opportunity to serve others, as you have and continue to do. In Jesus' name, Amen.

Day 21
I Think Big, I Dream Big, I Do Big

"For as he thinketh in his heart, so is he:"
Proverbs 23:7 KJV

Have you ever wondered, "What is my life's purpose?" or "Is there more to me?" Before God formed you in your mother's womb, He had a predestined purpose for your life. (Jer. 1:5 KJV) That purpose was inclusive of, but not limited to, motherhood. God's purpose for you will transform lives and reconcile hearts back to their first love- God! This will look different for each of us because God uses the good, bad, and the ugly in our lives to prepare and propel us into our purpose. Hear me, for where you are presently is not all you are. Ask God to reveal His plan for your life unto you. Ask Him to give you passion for your purpose. For it's His good pleasure to share His heart. I dare you to be all God created you to be!

Pray this:

Thank you Father, for transforming my mind into the mind of Christ. I rebuke the spirit of small thinking off of my mind and my subconscious. I choose to see myself through your lens. I am a woman of God and I will complete great feats for You, Father. I will move forward beyond fear, and walk in faith and courage. I will use the influence God has given me to encourage others to live their God-given purposes. May your glory be revealed to and through me! I dare to think big, dream big and do big, in Jesus' name, Amen.

~Author's Notes~

Although you have completed this 21 day devotional, I encourage you to continue to pray. Various topics within this book probably spoke directly and specifically to you. Add to the prayers I have shared within these pages, and tailor them to be the remedies to your needs. Remember to ask God for a scripture that applies, and to pray in faith. Truly, prayer changes things. Sometimes it happens overnight, and other times over months or even years; but know that God's timing is perfect and He is not done until everything is made good. Be encouraged to continue your faith journey and inspire others to do the same.

∞

~Here is Your Opportunity to Give Your Life to Jesus~

For some mothers, this 21 day devotional has fanned your passionate flame for prayer and for other mothers this may have been your first encounter with daily, focused prayer. I know that exposure creates appetite! If this is indeed your first encounter and you would like to give your life to Jesus Christ, to surrender your will for His, sincerely pray this prayer with me:

Jesus, I come before you in faith. I recognize that I am a sinner, and that I need you. You suffered. You died. You rose again to pay the ransom for my sins. Thank you for looking beyond my faults and loving me still. I confess with my mouth and believe in my heart that you are the Son of the living God, and by receiving you as my Lord and Savior, I have received the gift of salvation. As a child of God, I am saved by grace and free from sin and shame. I give you my life! Please lead and guide me to live a life pleasing unto you. In Jesus' name I pray, Amen.

Now that you have received Christ as your Savior, you are no longer a slave to sin. To grow stronger in your faith and deeper in God, get a Bible for yourself, read it daily, and ask God to reveal Himself to you through His Word. Also, find a Bible-based church that teaches the unfiltered Word of God. Take the Word of God as truth and apply it to your daily life.

Resources to assist you along this journey:

•**Online churches** have resources available from message archives to Bible Study materials. Here are two of my favorites:

-The Rock Church San Diego, CA
http://www.sdrock.com

-The Potter's House Dallas, TX
http://tdjakes.org/mobile/watch/live.php

•**Recommended books** to read: There are many wonderful books I can recommend, however here are two to get you started:

-The most important book of all, The **Holy Bible**. There are various translations available. I prefer the King James Version (KJV), New Living Translation (NLT), and the Amplified Version (AMP). *If cost is an issue, you can find used Bibles for sale online, in second-hand or thrift stores, and in some churches they are given out at no cost. The Bible Application is a handy resource as well. Be sure to download it from your mobile application store if you haven't already. You can also read the Bible and find different versions online at www.biblegateway.com.

-**Fervent: A Woman's Battle Plan for Serious, Strategic and Specific prayer**, by Priscilla Shirer. This book is available for sale at several local and online retailers.

~Author's Closing Thoughts~

I sincerely hope you prayed this prayer to give your life to Jesus if you have never done so before, or if you simply want to strengthen and deepen your Christian faith.

I pray that you will read the Word of God daily and find a good church where you can worship in community with other Christ followers, who will support you through your journey as a mother and a daughter of God. May you be blessed in all you do, and may your faith bless your children, family and other loved ones.

From one mother to another mother,

Genté Shaw